LAST ARK
OF THE RAILROAD

The Steam Ship *City of Milwaukee*—National Historic Landmark

DOMINIC R. SONDY

The Last Ark, The Steam Ship City of Milwaukee

Copyright © 2011 Dominic R. Sondy
All rights reserved.

Published by   Creative Aces Publishing, a division of Creative Aces Corporation;
                Chicago, Illinois

No part of this publication may be reproduced, stored in a retrieval system, or transmitted in any form or by any means, electronic, mechanical, photocopying, recording, scanning, or otherwise, except as permitted under Section 107 or 108 of the 1976 U.S. Copyright Act without the prior written permission of the publisher, Creative Aces Publishing. Requests to publisher for permission should be addressed to the Permissions Department, Creative Aces Publishing, 2144 N. Lincoln Park West #5B, Chicago, IL 60614, or by e-mail to publishing@creativeaces.com.

For informaion on discounts for bulk purchases, please Creative Aces Publishing, c/o publishing@creativeaces.com or wizard@vintageimage.biz

Publishers address and contact information
Visit our website at www.creativeaces.com or www.vintageimage.biz

ISBN-10: 0-9848950-0-0
ISBN-13: 978-0-9848950-0-7

Book Design by Creative Aces Corp.

First Edition: 07122011

While the author has made very effort to provide accurate telephone numbers and internet addresses at the time of publication, neither the publisher nor the author assumes any responsibility for errors, or for changes that occur after publication. Further, the publisher does not have any control over and does not assume any responsibility for author or third-party websites or their content.

TABLE OF CONTENTS

Foreword .... *VII*

The Backstory 1

On-Board Tour 9

    Cargo Deck 11

    Below Deck 13

    The Engine Room 17

Topside 33

Officer's Quarters & Bridge 43

Epilogue 57

Bibliography 58

About The Author 59

Foreword

The Steam Ship *City of Milwaukee* is a National Historic Landmark as well as a member of the Historic Naval Ship Association. Built at the beginning of the Great Depression, the *City of Milwaukee* shuttled railcars across Lake Michigan for over fifty years. She is currently moored in Manistee Michigan and is open to the public as a floating museum.

The *City of Milwaukee* is a fascinating time capsule. She is also the last of her kind. There are no railroad car ferries operating on the Great Lakes. The *City of Milwaukee* is in a superb state of preservation. This story serves as a testimonial to her service, to the people who work so hard to maintain her.

The Backstory

Railroad ferries regularly crossed the Great Lakes before cars, trucks or modern interstate highways existed. During the nineteenth century railroads had grown to the point of being the most efficient way to cross the country. There was a certain difficulty that accompanied the railroad's growing success. By the beginning of the twentieth century, the most efficient means to cross the continent had developed a traffic problem.

Railroad ferries were created to resolve one of the nation's first, and largest, examples of gridlock. Chicago was where the nation's railroads converged, making it the hub of the country's transportation system. Manufactured goods and fuel from the east passed through Chicago on their way to western destinations. Agricultural products, from the Midwest, were directed through Chicago. Beef, from the southwest came to Chicago, was processed and sent back out again to be distributed nationally through the rail system. Passenger trains were also part of the mix. Trains moving people were forced to slow-down while passing through Chicago's traffic-jam. Freight trains usually just stopped; they had to wait while the passenger trains passed. Sometimes entire freight trains became lost in the maze of switching yards adjacent to Chicago. Locating a lost train, and sending it on its way, could take as long as a week. There was a huge "means of access" problem plaguing the very center of the entire national railroad network. The railroads implemented a pragmatic solution: Rail car ferries simply circumvented the clogged-up pinch-point.

The *Steam Ship Milwaukee* was one of the first generation Lake Michigan railcar ferries. She carried rail freight across Lake Michigan. Grand Haven Michigan and Milwaukee Wisconsin were her ports of call.

A liquidity crisis made October 1929 a disastrous month for the U.S. Stock market; a huge portion of America's work force suffered the consequences. Another kind of liquidity crisis evolved into the ultimate problem for the microcosm of American laborers on the *Steam Ship Milwaukee*; they too suffered severe consequences. The stock market crashed, and the *S.S. Milwaukee* sank, on October 29, 1929.

On that ill-fated October day the Steam Ship *Grand Haven*, one of the oldest ships in the rail-ferry fleet, left Milwaukee at 2:00 a.m. She arrived in Grand Haven, Michigan at 5:00 p.m. The sixty-mile trip usually took six hours to complete. The old ship had steamed, almost head-on, into a gale. Thirty-seven mile per hour winds, blowing out of the northeast nearly tripled the old ferry's usual time. The *Steam Ship Milwaukee* left the same port early in the afternoon of that historic day. She had no radio and was never heard from again.

A Coast Guard patrolman later found her watertight message case. It contained a hand-written note:

> *The ship is taking water fast. We have turned around and headed for Milwaukee. Pumps are working but sea gate is bent in and can't keep the water out. Flicker is flooded. Seas are tremendous. Things look bad. Crew roll is about the same as on last payday.*
> A.R. Sadon, Purser

There were somewhere between 46 and 53 people (the purser's message hadn't accounted for passengers) on board the *S.S. Milwaukee*. Twenty-one bodies were recovered. The ship was valued at $600,000 and had about $120,000 worth of cargo on board when she went down.

The Grand Trunk Western Railroad immediately began building a new and improved ship at the yards in Manitowoc Wisconsin. The new ship's design was similar to the *Ann Arbor*

Number Seven, built six years earlier. Her steel hull, number 261, was just short of 348 feet long and just over 56 feet wide. Four Scotch boilers developed 185 pounds of steam pressure to power her two triple expansion engines. "Triple expansion" means that the force of expanding steam was used three times to push a series of three successively lager pistons. The first piston and cylinder combination was 20 and one half inches in diameter. The expanding steam pressure then moved to drive a 34-inch piston. A 56-inch piston/cylinder set was the end of the line for the steam's final power thrust. The combined output of the *City of Milwaukee*'s steam engines totaled 2,700 horsepower. This was enough to move her across Lake Michigan at a top speed of 14 miles per hour.

A bottle of milk (in keeping with national prohibition) was broken on her bow when the ship was launched on November 25, 1930. The new ship was named the *City of Milwaukee*. The "City of" prefix was added to her name to disassociate her form her ill-fated predecessor. She started making regular runs across Lake Michigan in January. The biggest, and most noticeable, improvement over the *S.S. Milwaukee* was her larger and sturdier sea gate.

The sea gate is a huge steel clamshell door on the ship's stern. This immense door is only open while railroad cars are loaded onto or off of the ship. The *City of Milwaukee*'s cargo hold is a cavernous space with four sets of railroad tracks attached to its floor. Each set of tracks is long enough to hold eight rail cars. These cars were usually flat cars, boxcars or an occasional tank car. The *City of Milwaukee* was designed for hauling rolling stock in her hold. It never carried automobiles (unless they were secured to rail cars) or had loose freight lashed down in her hold. Since rail cars were pushed on and pulled off, the flat and level rear deck was fairly close to the surface of the water. The closed sea gate would prevent waves from washing over the ship's stern, flooding the hull and sinking the ship.

The *City of Milwaukee* was able to go into service in January, when large portions of Lake Michigan were frozen, because her massive steel hull carried a lot of weight. Railroad car ferries were among the first icebreaking ships. The *City of Milwaukee* could easily force her way, head-on, through ice three feet thick. Maneuvering in an ice-clogged port was another matter. Ice, combined with limited space to maneuver, were the reasons her Michigan port was switched from Grand Haven to Muskegon in 1933.

The *S.S. City of Milwaukee* had a supporting role during World War II. She carried enough war materials across Lake Michigan to earn registry as a member of the Historic Naval Ship Association.

In 1946 The *City of Milwaukee* moved north one more time, to Frankfort Michigan. Frankfort and Muskegon are similar ports because each is situated on a large inland lake and is connected to Lake Michigan by a short deep channel. Unlike Muskegon, Frankfort had the advantage of an alternate berthing site, on the lake's opposite shore, in Elberta Michigan. Later that year, the Grand Trunk Railroad abandoned its direct rail line to Muskegon.

> By mid-twentieth century railroads, along with their floating rail fleet, had reached their commercial zenith. The number of Great Lake ferries peaked with as many as eighty ships ferrying railroad cars, passengers and automobiles across all of the five Great Lakes.

Several regular routes crossed the Lake Michigan. Multiple ferries also linked Michigan's upper and lower peninsulas. After achieving this high point, ferry traffic went into a steady decline.

The biggest reason for railroad ferries obsolescence: the pinch-point, at Chicago, no longer needed to be circumvented. The original reason for establishing the rail ferry system was no longer valid. Improved methods for processing meat, relocating the processing plants closer to their source of supply, meant that Chicago's stockyards also were no longer necessary. The

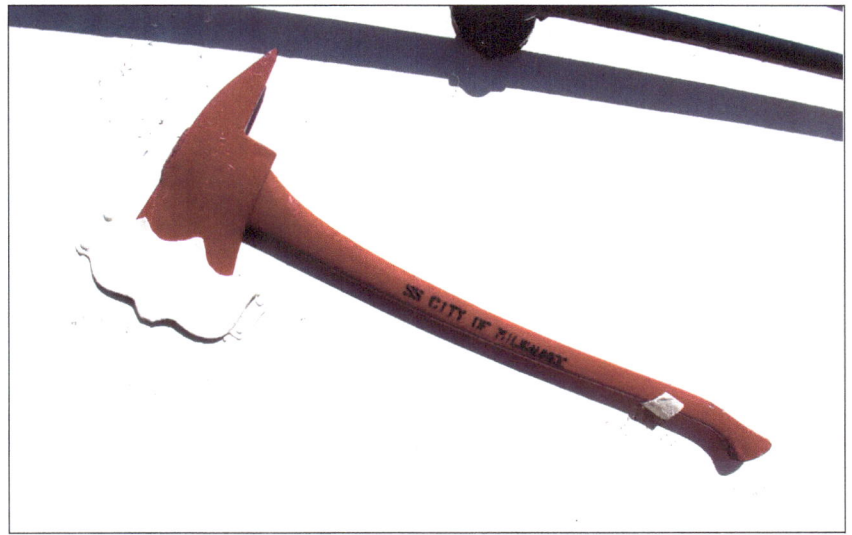

stockyards, along with the acreage that once was used for switching yards, were eventually dismantled. The land was transformed into neighborhoods and suburbs.

The end of the Korean War marked the beginning of a construction boom. This national growth had an inverse effect on railroads.

The single largest national building project: a brand new world-class system of inter-state highways. Trucks, using those highways, went into direct competition with the railroads for hauling freight. Post-war prosperity presented more Americans with the opportunity to buy automobiles and drive them on the new highways. Airliners travel became safer. Passenger rail usage took a steep nosedive. Additionally, the completion of a new bridge, connecting the straights of Mackinaw in Michigan, resulted in even more ferries being put out of business. The results of these combined circumstances translated into grim news for railroads in general and was especially catastrophic for rail ferries. The dynamics of transportation in the United States had changed and that change precipitated the demise of rail ferries.

In 1979 the Grand Trunk and Western Railroad wanted to eliminate its ferry service. They leased the *City of Milwaukee* to a company which planned to use her as part of a two-ship operation. This new company was purposed to ferry rail cars between Manitowoc Wisconsin and Frankfort Michigan. Two ships were all that were necessary to fill a need that had, thirty years earlier, kept many ships working. The once flourishing rail ferry era was just about over. The nearly fifty-year old *City of Milwaukee* was enlisted to do double duty while another ship was being refitted to work with her. There was a problem on her very first run.

The *City of Milwaukee* had already crossed Lake Michigan, and had cleared the channel into Frankfort, when ice prevented her from backing into her slip. The fully loaded ship backed her way out of port, through the channel and into the open waters of Lake Michigan where she waited for the ice to be cleared. The problem was that the ship's crew, knowing that they were in port, had started preparations to unload their cargo. They had released some of the jacks that prevented the railcars from rolling around while they were crossing the lake. Now they were out in the lake, again, and riding large swells rolling across Lake Michigan. Two of the recently unsecured rail cars moved. Worse yet, they tipped over. One car only partly tipped. It came to rest leaning against a wall near the bow and was easily righted. The second car completely tipped over and spilled 170 tons of potash onto the deck. There was no way to stand the car back up onto its wheels until all of that potash was cleaned out. It took two weeks to clean up the mess and repair the damage. The City of Milwaukee was supposed to cross the lake twice every twenty-four hours. Lost revenue, clean up and repairs did not mark an auspicious start for the *City of Milwaukee*'s new venture.

The ship that was to have been the other half of the original two-ship deal needed more time, than expected, for its refit. The work was eventually completed; but a third ship had been brought in to fill the backlog created by starting with only one ship. The two-ship deal had turned into a three-ship deal: the *Viking*, the

Arthur K. Atkinson and the *City of Milwaukee* became the last three railroad ferries crossing Lake Michigan. The *City of Milwaukee* was the oldest and slowest of the three; by 1982 her age and speed didn't really matter. At that point, any ship was one ship too many. The railroad had cut down its schedule and was running one train every other day. That schedule couldn't sustain one ship, much less three. All three ships were moved from Frankfort, across the inland lake, to Elberta, Michigan. The *Viking* and the *Atkinson* were put up for sale in October 1982 and eventually sold.

The citizens of Frankfort Michigan bought the *City of Milwaukee* on December 13, 1984. They paid one dollar for the ship. She moved back across the lake, to Elberta, in 1985. The people of Frankfort doubled their money. They sold their ship to the Society for the Preservation of the *City of Milwaukee* in October of 1988 for two dollars. She achieved landmark status in 1990 and moved to Manistee Michigan May 18, 2004.

The *City of Milwaukee* had been built at the onset of the Great Depression. She is a still afloat today and welcomes visitors in her current incarnation as a floating museum.

On Board Tour

Cargo Deck

Visitors board the *City of Milwaukee* the same way her cargo came on board: over the stern. They walk up a slightly inclined ramp, pass under her permanently raised Sea Gate and are immediately rewarded with an impressive view into the ship's immense cargo bay. This cavernous space is a mostly empty. The Cargo bay is over a football field long and more than fifty feet wide. Steel walls, painted white, support the broad expanse of ceiling towering more than twenty feet overhead. The rear portion of the ship is fairly well lit, thanks to the natural light flooding through the open sea gate. The bow is an elusive vertical line far off in the shadowy distance. There are four sets of railroad tracks attached to the cargo bay deck. Elevated wooden walkways make walking over the tracks a little easier. These wooden sidewalks are lined with informative historical exhibits and lead to a few remaining boxcars. The boxcars doors are open. Steps take visitors up from the walkway into the railcars that have been converted into a gift shop, mini-theater and more exhibit space. The small number of boxcars in the *City of Milwaukee*'s hold emphasizes the scale of her spacious cargo bay and how much more room is still available to park more railcars.

Crew's Quarters

Crew Hygiene Station

Below Decks

Visitors, exploring the area below the *City of Milwaukee*'s cargo deck, must first go through the crew's quarters. After a short descent down some narrow steps, guests enter a wide room. The proportions of the space create the illusion of an unusually low ceiling. Bulkheads, with watertight doors, delineate the fore and aft ends of the room. This is the crew's common area. It is well lit and clean. Two massive steel columns divide the room into three equal parts. The columns once supported the weight of the loaded railcars overhead as well as the steel ceiling that is the underside of the cargo bay floor. A big wooden picnic-style table is bolted to the deck between the columns. This is where the crew could read or play cards while not working. The walls on either side of the room are lined with doors that lead into the crew sleeping compartments. Each of these small side rooms has a set of bunk beds, two lockers and a bench. Communal toilets and showers are also accessed through doorways on the sidewalls.

A hygiene station, in the form of a series of sinks and mirrors, is located on the rear bulkhead. Passing rearward, through its watertight bulkhead door, guests find themselves in a workshop. The shop has a sturdy steel surfaced worktable, littered with assorted tools. The shop also has various floor-mounted power tools. Harsh work lights are focused on the work areas, leaving the walls and corners in shadow.

Past the workshop compartment, in the very back of the ship's stern, are the mechanisms that move the ship's massive rudders. There isn't much light in this space; the source of the modest illumination comes from bare-bulbs. Their glaring light reveals rusted steel surfaces and creates contrasting deep dark shadows that keep the room's mysterious recesses hidden from sight

Below Deck Crew's Quarters

Worm-Drive Gear

Rudder Control Gear

This is a surreal place. Power steering on steroids has been somehow crammed into an impossibly small space. A pair of massive toothed gears, coated in thick black grease, dominates either side of this compartment.

    The horizontal gears are attached to vertical shafts. These shafts turn the ship's rudders. This area was never intended to be pretty or seen by the public. It was made to work, without fail, for fifty years. It is also a dead-end.

    Visitors have to go back, through the workshop and the crew's quarters, to reach the bulkhead door that leads to the Engine Room.

Engine Room

Passing through this portal visitors find a remarkable labyrinth of pipes, valves, wires and gauges. They are now located just aft of mid-ship, still under the deck of the cargo hold, and are totally immersed in a dense three-dimensional mechanical maze of levers, pipelines, electrical conduits and structural supports. Metal-grate flooring, on multiple levels, is connected by steep metal stairways. At the very bottom guests find a solid steel deck, with grated openings providing drainage into the ship's bilge. Two sets of three mammoth connecting rods link the engine's steam driven pistons to two crankshafts.

These drive crankshafts are connected to exposed propeller shafts. The drive shafts run, through the *City of Milwaukee*'s stern and terminate at the ship's big, twelve foot diameter, iron screws. The massive propeller shafts are supported, at several points, by huge bearings. The shafts, and their bearings, are exposed because they had to be accessible for maintenance. The bearings were lubricated by hand. This meant that, when the ship was moving, the crew had to carefully step over the big turning shafts while walking on an often slippery and pitching deck.

> *Excess lubricants and fluids often spilled onto the deck. They eventually drained into the ship's bilge, where they collected, and were pumped out, over the side, by large high-output bilge pumps. This entire operation is below the ship's waterline.*

There are no portholes to let in natural light; yet, this place is not dark. Two large steam-powered Direct Current generators used to provide all of the ship's electricity; apparently lighting the engineroom was a priority. These dynamos are connected to an imposing 1930's style black enamel control panel. Looking like a prop from a Frankenstein movie, this impressive array of dials and switches monitored both of the generators power production

Steam Powered Direct Current Generator

as well as distributed their electrical output throughout the ship. Today electrical power comes through a cable connected to a power source on shore.

The Engine Room was designed with huge amounts of ventilation. Circulating air was needed for the ship's boiler fires and to cool the space; otherwise the crew would have been soggy toast. The combination of plentiful light and fresh air keeps this enclosed space from feeling claustrophobic.

The *City of Milwaukee*'s engine room is over eighty years old. The engines haven't run for almost thirty years; but there is very little rust or dust. Instead, there is cosmolene. It covers everything, including the crew's antique wringer washing machine.

Crew's Laundry

Electrical Control Panel

Cosmolene is a brownish/orange substance that is a cross between wax and grease. It is used to prevent metal from rusting. When it is fresh cosmolene is sticky. When it is twenty years old cosmolene hardens into a matte finished glaze. It eventually chips off in flakes, taking the top layer of paint with it. So the *City of Milwaukee*'s Engine Room is a little "flakey" and does not appear as ship-shape as it might have once been. The old ship no longer has a full-time engine room crew working 24/ seven keeping it ship shape. Instead, dedicated volunteers work all over the ship.

These volunteers maintain the whole ship. They work tirelessly cleaning, polishing and maintaining the *City of Milwaukee*. Dedicated people also work to up-grade some of the older systems.

The *City of Milwaukee*'s boilers no longer produce steam to power her generators. Two generators easily produced enough DC current to run the ship. Now, the ship uses more common alternating current; from a dockside hook-up. The entire ship has been re-wired to accommodate AC power.

> *The Engine Room is a place of pre-WWII mechanical marvels. It is crammed with gadgets that have inquisitive visitors asking tour guides about the functions of all the fascinating valves, levers and stuff.*

The ship's guides have an encyclopedic knowledge of their ship and are eagar to answer questions. Their explanations are informational, logical and maintain a historic context. One frequently asked question: *"How did the engine room, down here, communicate with the people navigating the ship, up there?"*

Engine Room Ship's Order Telegraph

On Board Tour

It isn't hard to imagine how loud it must have been in the engine room. Steam pistons pumping, prop shafts turning and two big propellers pushing the massive hull through rolling swells or creaking ice. The cacophony must have been continuous and immensely distracting, Communication with the Captain and officers topside must have been, at the very least, difficult.

Redundant systems were used, to pass along the Captain's orders. Multiple Engine Order Telegraphs served as a mechanical means of communication. Two sets of these devises, one fore and another aft, were located topside. These were physically linked, via cables and pulleys, to the engine room. Engine Order Telegraphs look something like brass clocks mounted on pedestals and were bolted to the floor of the Bridge and the stern wheelhouse. A handle, with a pointer, would be moved around the outer

Engine Room Steam Control Valves

Engine Room Gauges and Controls

Engine Room Gauge Detail

circumference of each telegraph. The location of the pointer on the topside devise was telegraphed to an identical devise in the engine room. The position of a pointer indicated which command, inscribed on the telegraph's face, was to be implemented.

> *The City of Milwaukee did not use tugboats to maneuver while she was in port. The Captain walked to the stern pilot-station, where he personally backed the big ship into her dock.*

Another intra-ship communication system came in the analog form of speaking tubes. This holdover from the nineteenth century had no moving parts. Officers on the bridge would simply shout into a funnel, connected to a tube. The tube carried commands down to the engine room. Modern telephones provided a third connection to the engine room. Apparently vocal communication over these phones wasn't very loud. Therefore, in

Another Engine Room Gauge

Engine Room Detail

Engine Room Telephonic Communication Station

consideration of all the noise below decks, the engine room has an enclosed three-man-sized phone booth.

Today noise is not a problem for guests. They find it easy to hear docents while touring the *City of Milwaukee* because there is very little noise. It is very quiet on board the ship. It is almost too quiet.

The nearly absolute silence on this floating museum is downright eerie. The crypt-like quiet is disturbed by unexpected metallic clicks, groans and pings. Unusual noises suddenly ring-out and echo through the ship's empty compartments. Unexplained sounds reverberate so much that it is impossible to know where they originated in the huge ship. Some parts of the *City of Milwaukee*'s metal hull are cooling, and contracting, in the shade while other parts are heating-up and expanding in the sunlight. The *City of Milwaukee* pings, creaks and moans, display an auditory spooky side that startles some unprepared guests. In fact, these *surprising* sounds are so creepy that the Preservation Society presents visitors with special Halloween night tours.

The boilers are located in front of the engine compartment. A bulkhead door, leading into the boiler room itself, is permanently sealed shut.

Past her boilers, in the bow (but still below the cargo deck), are the compartments where the anchor chain is stored as well as the mechanisms for raising and lowering the anchors. Like the rudder assemblies in the stern, these machines were not designed for beauty. These devices are even bigger and more powerful than the rudder mechanisms. The forward compartments are also the place where the stairs leading down into the bilge are located. The ship's keel, all of her ribs and the inside of her bottom sheathing are revealed at the end of the steep steel steps.

Guests ascend another set of steps that take them back into the Cargo Bay. Near the place where their below deck tour started, visitors find the only means for going topside: another set of stairs; these are much longer.

Stair Leading to the Bilge

Engine Room Mechanical Details

Chain Locker

Engine Room Chainfall

Topside

Ascending from the Cargo Bay, guests emerge into the fresh air on the ship's main deck, just behind the main cabin. Railings run along either side of a wide expansive deck. This open space separates the main cabin structure from a relatively small rear-facing wheelhouse perched on the ship's stern. A big black mechanical wench is mounted in the center of this otherwise empty deck space.

The City of Milwaukee ferried passengers along with railcars. The areas dedicated to the passengers are situated in the forward section of the main cabin.

There are plenty of entrances into the main cabin. Passengers would have probably walked about halfway along the outside and entered the cabin through one of the side doors; the crew would have entered through the back door.

Radio Shack

Passenger's Dining Room

The communications room is located, off to one side, inside the backdoor crew entrance. Continuing forward guests view three separate dining areas: the Crew's Mess, the Officer's Dining room, and the Passenger's Dining room. The Passenger's Dining Room, with its ventilated ceiling skylights, is airy and almost luxurious compared to the crew's cramped accommodations.

Visitors can see the pantry, food preparation area, as well as the walk-in refrigerator before entering the Galley. The compartments connected to the Galley are all compact rooms, with just enough space allotted for their dedicated purposes.

> *The galley is a slightly larger space dominated by a huge black cast iron coal-burning stove. This bad-boy is not your regular kitchen appliance; it is a BIG cooking machine.*

The flat broad cook top is fenced-in by heavy rails. The stove's sturdy guardrails prohibited big pots from tipping in rolling seas as well as prevented the cook from accidentally being pitched onto the griddle.

Crew's Mess

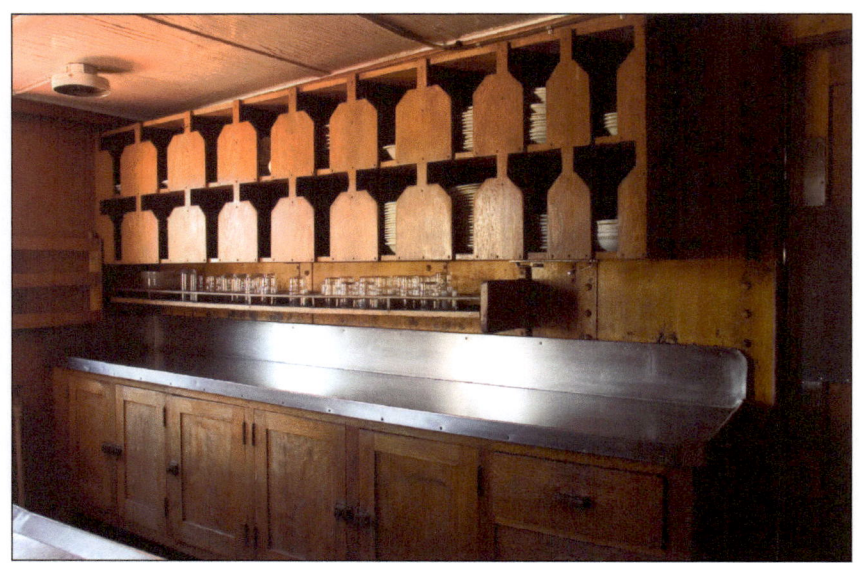

China and Cutlery Pantry

Coal-fired Stove

Food Preparation Area

This cast-iron behemoth of cookery is festooned, on its front, with several heavy metal doors: oven doors, doors to stoke its fires and more doors to empty the ashes. The stove also has its own fire prevention system as well as a smokestack. The person using this piece of equipment could have easily been referred to as a "Heavy Equipment Operator" as opposed his better-known title of "Cook".

The main passenger promenade is located in front of the Galley. It is a wide bright hallway lined with passenger cabins, a Smoking Lounge, the Purser's Office and the Nurses station/stateroom. An arts and crafts style bench is an attractive feature on the portside wall. The main Passenger's Lounge is located at the most forward end of the promenade.

The Passenger Lounge has six panoramic windows offering views of the front deck and horizons beyond. Chairs appearing to

Officer's Dining Room

Promenade Deck

Promenade Deck Seating

On Board Tour 39

Passenger's Lounge

be wicker, are actually hemp, provide seating. They are attached to the walls to keep them from sliding around the tilting deck. A clock, mounted on one of the Lounge's oak paneled walls, is of the spring-wound variety, even though an electric model was available.

At first glance the accommodations provided in the passenger cabins appear rather Spartan.

Remember, the *City of Milwaukee* was a ferry. She was only four hours between ports twice a day. The staterooms were used mostly on her night runs and weren't designed for luxury or extended stays. Even with this in mind, there are some larger "adjoining" cabins but most are small rooms with bunk beds. The smallest staterooms are like railroad sleeper car compartments with fold-up Pullman-style upper bunk beds. Each room has a small sink, porthole window and a little hinged folding seat attached to the wall. The seat was provided so guests could tie their shoes

Purser's Office

Dispensary & Nurse's Quarters

without having to sit on the bed and putting their feet on the bedding. The bathrooms were public.

The Purser was the ships clerk. His office had a barred window that opened onto the promenade deck. He had a stateroom that adjoined his office.

Clock - Passenger's Lounge

The ship's nurse was probably the only female crew member on the *City of Milwaukee*. Her stateroom/office is located on the promenade deck near the Purser's Office. It does not have bunk beds. However, the nurse's stateroom did have an additional bed, it was intended for an infirmed passenger or crewmember.

Adjoining Passenger Staterooms

Officer's Quarters & Bridge

The deck above the passenger area is where the Officer's Quarters are located. The Captain's Quarters are directly over the forward passenger lounge. His room has four forward-facing panoramic windows, similar to the passengers lounge. He had even better views than the passengers because his room was a little higher; the Captain could see over the rails and the forward deck wench. Despite the best view, compared to any stateroom on the ship, the Captain's quarters were the source of some consternation. The Grand Trunk Railroad built and owned the *City of Milwaukee*. They didn't know, or understand, that ship's Captains are very special people. They are to be treated as super-stars and expect (demand) respect as well as very plush accommodations. The Captain's quarters on the *City of Milwaukee* are not plush. They are, far and away, the most austere rooms of any Captain on the Great

Captain's Quarters

Captain's Quarters

Lakes and were hardly acceptable. Fortunately, the Captain never had to sleep in them. Unlike the rest of the crew, Captains were not required to live on board.

All of the other officers had their quarters on the same level as the Captain. Their accommodations were somewhat better than the crew quarters below decks. Officers enjoyed the advantages of relative quiet, fresh air and sunlight. A well-worn stairway, leading up to the bridge, separates the Captain's quarters from his officers.

The crow's nest sports the best view on the entire ship. It is the highest point on the City of Milwaukee and is located on a short mast, almost fifty feet above the water, just behind the bridge. Visitors are discouraged from climbing up there.

The Bridge has the second best view on the ship and visitors are encouraged to spend time there. The limited space within the Wheelhouse is dominated by the ship's classic wooden steering wheel. A polished brass compass binnacle is mounted to the floor

Junior Officer's Quarters

Stair Leading to Pilot Room

The Chadburn

Wheel House and Gauges

in front of the wheel. The Ship Order Telegraph, connected to an identical instrument in the engine room, is mounted to the floor within easy reach to the left (Port) side of the wheel. The Chadburn Company manufactured ship order telegraphs. Their reputation for making ship order telegraphs supplied the devise with a nickname. It was simply referred to as the Chadburn. A second telegraph is mounted to the floor on the starboard side of the Bridge. This devise is about setting the ship's course. Engine room speaking tubes are attached to the port sidewall along with the telephone.

There is no place to sit on the bridge and barely enough room for more than three men to stand.

A tall chart table, with multiple storage drawers, is located on the rear wall. Electronic navigation and radio equipment, that had been state-of-the-art forty years ago, is mounted the ceiling over the chart table.

Wheel and Controls

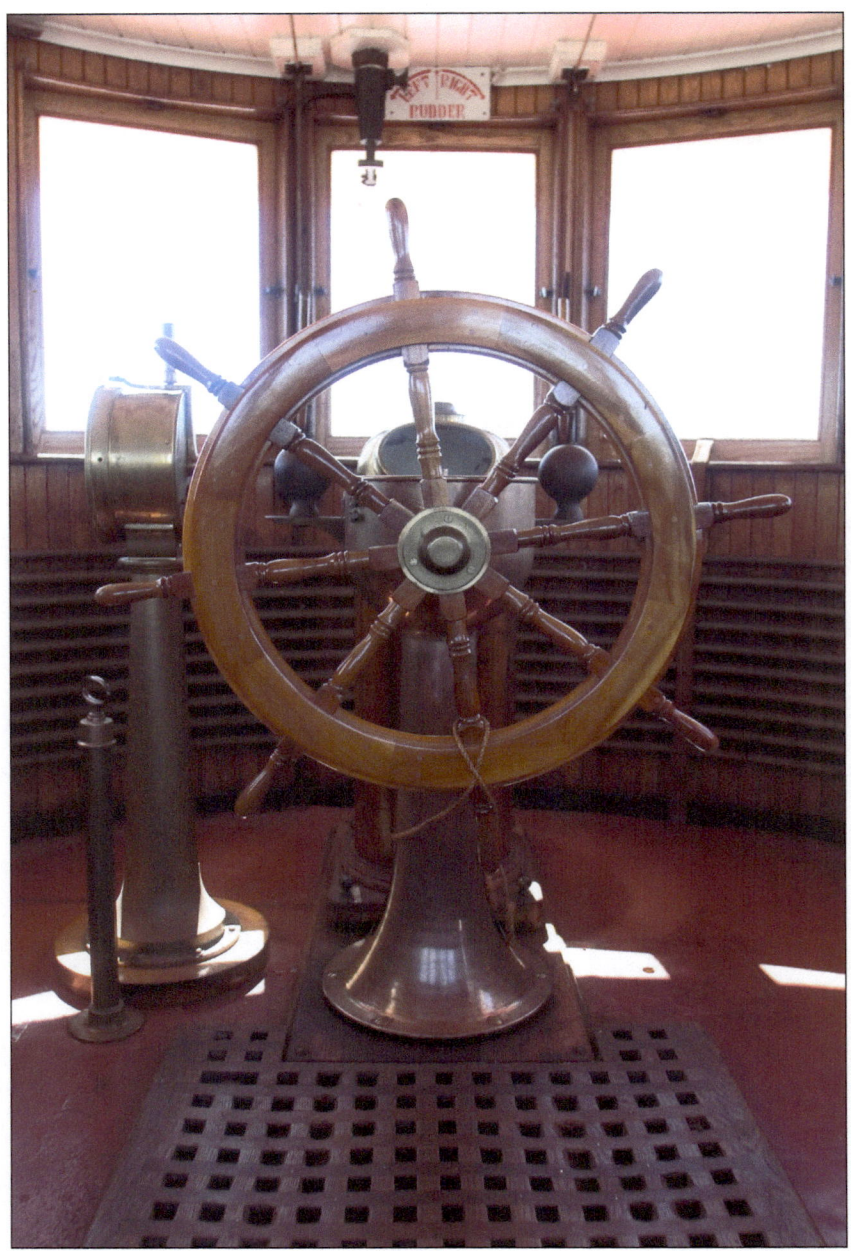

The Ship's Wheel

At first, it seems amazing that a ship of this size could be controlled from such a small room. The mechanical controls seem so modest, uncomplicated and so few in number. Applying that train of thought to the stern wheelhouse makes operating the ship from that point even more remarkable. The stern wheelhouse is where the Captain backed the ship up to the dock. The physical space of that room is a bit larger than the Bridge. But the stern wheelhouse has even fewer instruments and controls than the Bridge. Yet the Captain was able to maneuver the *City of Milwaukee*, with enough precision, to match-up his on board rail tracks with those on shore. He often performed this intricate docking drill in the dark of night and sometimes under adverse weather conditions.

On their way down from the Bridge guests are invited to revisit areas of interest. During their return to the steps leading down into the cargo bay they can pick-out details they might have initially missed. For example, the last Captain left his personal radio on a shelf in his cabin or one of the officers forgot a little tin of licorice wafers, that he propped-up on his shaving mug, in his quarters. After all, this is time capsule. There are so many little fine points that could be inadvertently overlooked. It is almost impossible to comprehend everything in just one trip. The *City of Milwaukee* is certainly the kind of place you would want to come back to again.

Rear Wheelhouse Engine Order Telegraphs

Captain's Personal Radio

On Board Tour

Forward Deck Winch

Epilog

Information about touring the *City of Milwaukee*'s decks, touching her rich oak paneled cabin walls and experiencing her rugged majesty is available at: www.carferry.com.

In the backstory, it is noted that *Steam Ship Milwaukee* left port and "was never heard from again." Originally the phrase "never was seen again" was used. This was changed because "never seen" is not entirely accurate. Scuba divers do indeed visit the *City of Milwaukee*'s predecessor. She sits on the bottom of Lake Michigan in 150 feet of water. Her cargo of railcars spilled out of her broken sea gate during her descent and are scattered around her. The Steam Ship Milwaukee is accessible; but the combination of cold and deep-water mandates very limited visiting times and makes a visit to the wreck of the SS Milwaukee an altogether different sort of adventure. More information about the *SS Milwaukee* is available through the Underwater Archaeological Society of Chicago at: www.uaschicago.org.

Railroad ferries no longer cross Lake Michigan. However, as of this writing, two seasonal automotive/ passenger ferries are still making the crossing.

The *Steam Ship Badger* was built in 1953 at the very apex of the "Golden Age" of Great Lakes ferries. As of this writing, she seasonally makes regular crossings between Manitowoc, Wisconson and Ludington, Michigan. The largest Great Lakes ferry ever built, 410 feet long, the *Badger* is currently the object of considerable controversy. Apparently it is the only coal-fired ship still operating in North America and will have to convert to a more environmentally-friendly fuel or stop operations. For more information about the *Badger*'s current status, or the possibility of taking the four hour sentimental journey, visit her website: www.ssbadger.com.

The *Lake Express* is a faster alternative for traveling between Milwaukee Wisconsin and Muskegon Michigan. This 192 foot long twin hull ferry, launched in 2004, makes the trip in just two ½ hours. Four diesel engines power the Lake Expess' water jet propulsion system, enabling her to reach a cruising speed of forty miles per hour. Information about flying across the surface of Lake Michigan can be found at: www.lake-express.com.

Bibliography

NINTY YEARS CROSSING LAKE MICHIGAN, The History of the Ann Arbor Car Ferries by Grant Brown Jr. Published by the University of Michigan Press

THE GREAT LAKES CAR FERRIES by George W. Hilton Published by Howell-North Berkley CA 1962

About The Author

Dominic R. Sondy has spent most of his career behind the lens documenting events, locations, people and a variety of subjects. Dominic is somewhat knowledgeable in Adobe Photoshop. His combined technical skills help provide powerful results for clients. His background includes Chief Photographer with one of the nation's most respected tradeshow photography companies. He was a member of the *Chicago Tribune* advertising sales staff and was a Correspondent for the U.S. Army in Vietnam.

Digital illustration is a detail-oriented process requiring skill and patience. It is not a Photoshop filter or some kind of computer plug-in. The techniques and tools used to create a digital illustration are similar to those used to make an illustration with pen and ink.

Visit the Vintage Image website (www.vintageimage.biz) to purchase images presented in this book or see some of the other collections including:

Can't See The Forest Through The Trees — Aborial reflections.
Used Buggy Parts — An satirical introduction to "automotive entomolgy".
Great Lakes Maritime — Tall ships, USCG ships & boats, tugs, car ferries and more.
New Orleans' Garden District — Beautiful study of this historic neighborhood.
Coleman's Trolley — Views of the city in decay as seen from Detroit's People Mover.
Saigon Shuffle — Images from Dominic's Vietnam memoir" available in softcover and ebook.
Classic Car Hood Ornaments and Emblems — Museum quality cars and parts.

VICTORY
Articulated Tug
Menominee, Michigan

Dominic R. Sondy 2009

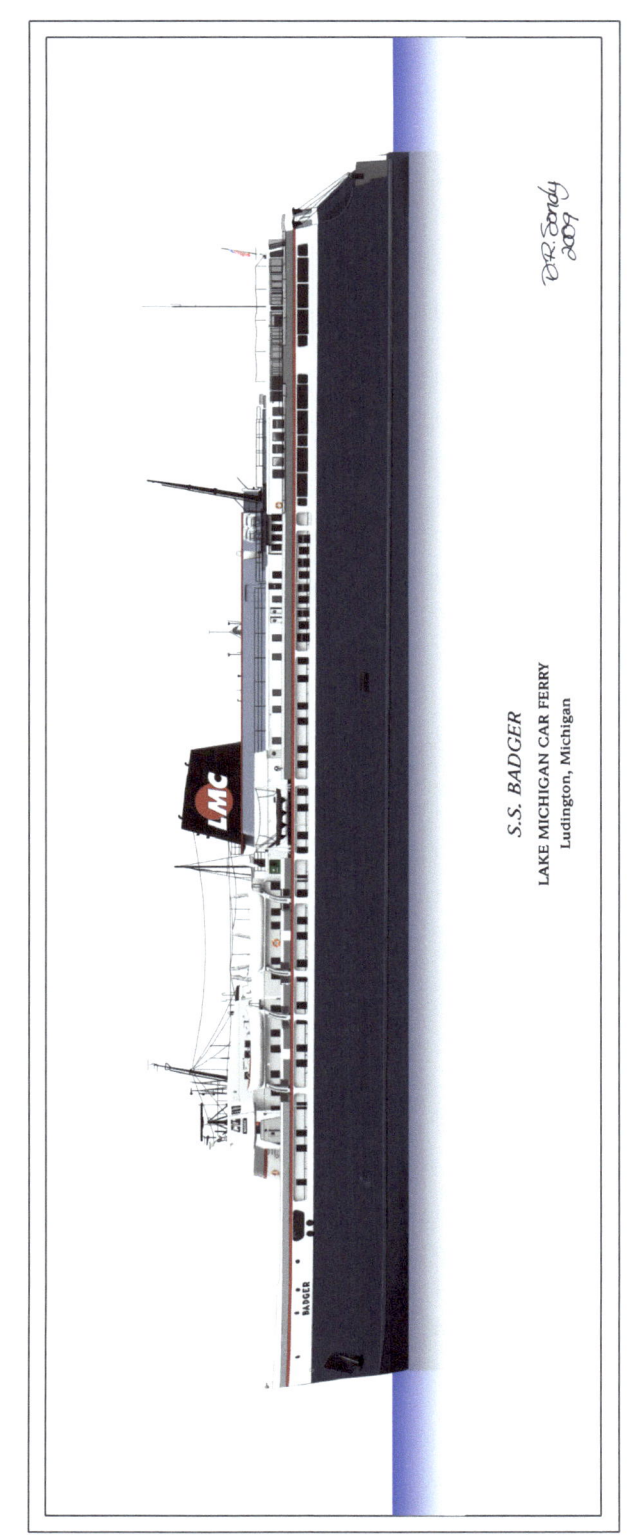

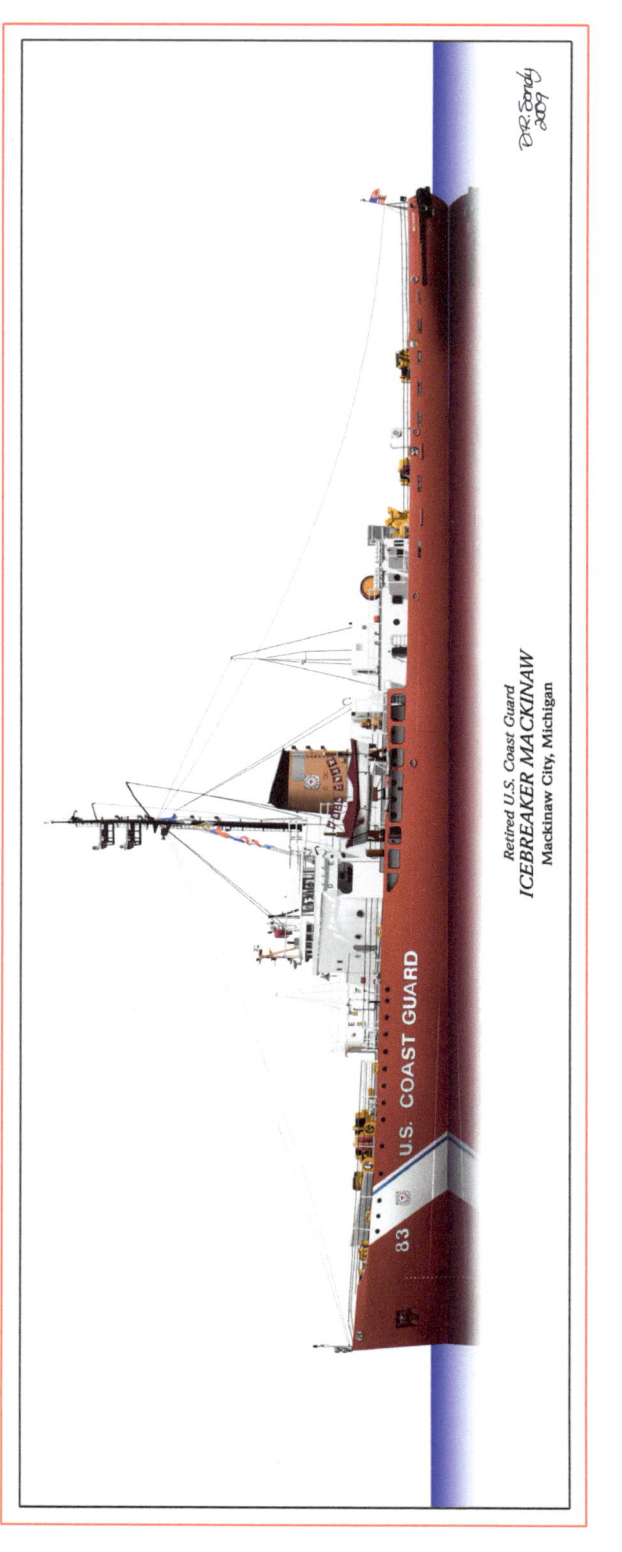

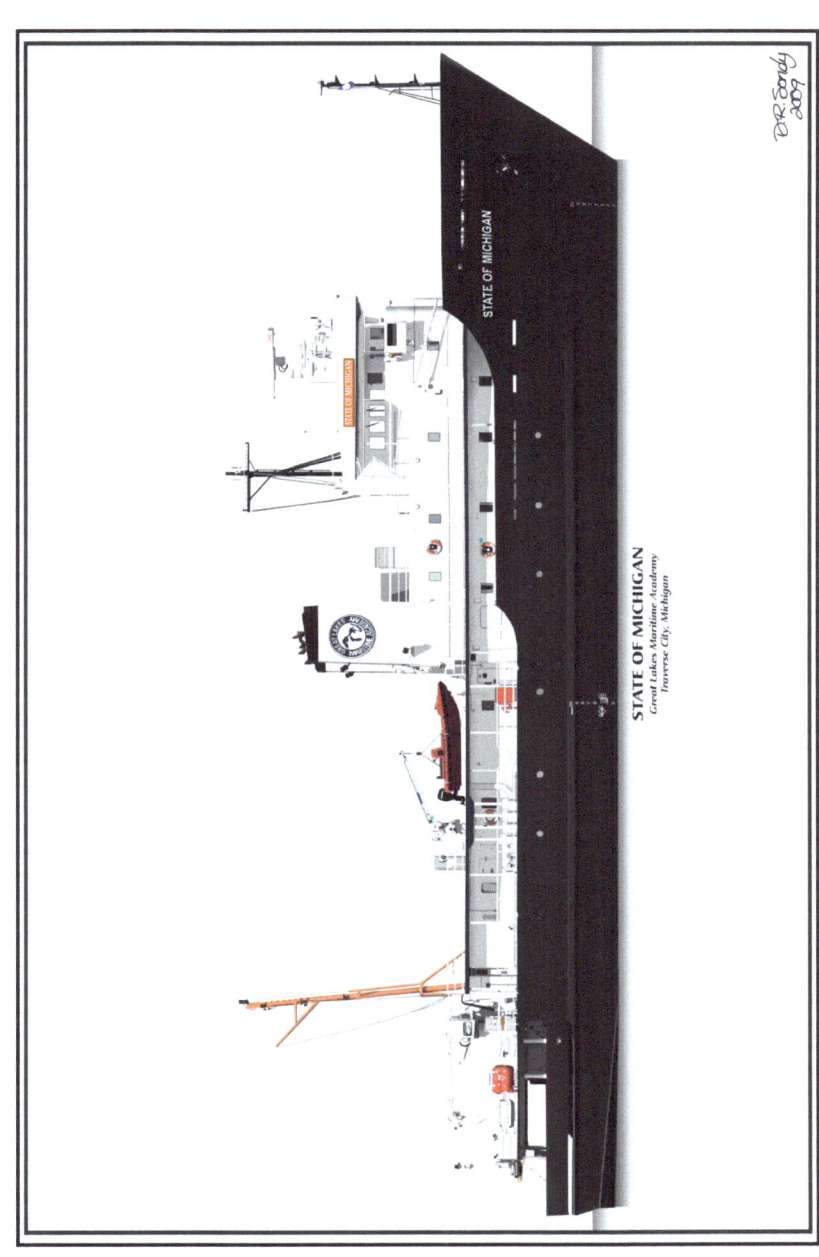

STATE OF MICHIGAN
Great Lakes Maritime Academy
Traverse City, Michigan

BOB LO EXCURSION STEAMER
STE CLAIRE
BUILT 1910 BY DETROIT DRY DOCK
DESIGNED BY FRANK E. KIRBY

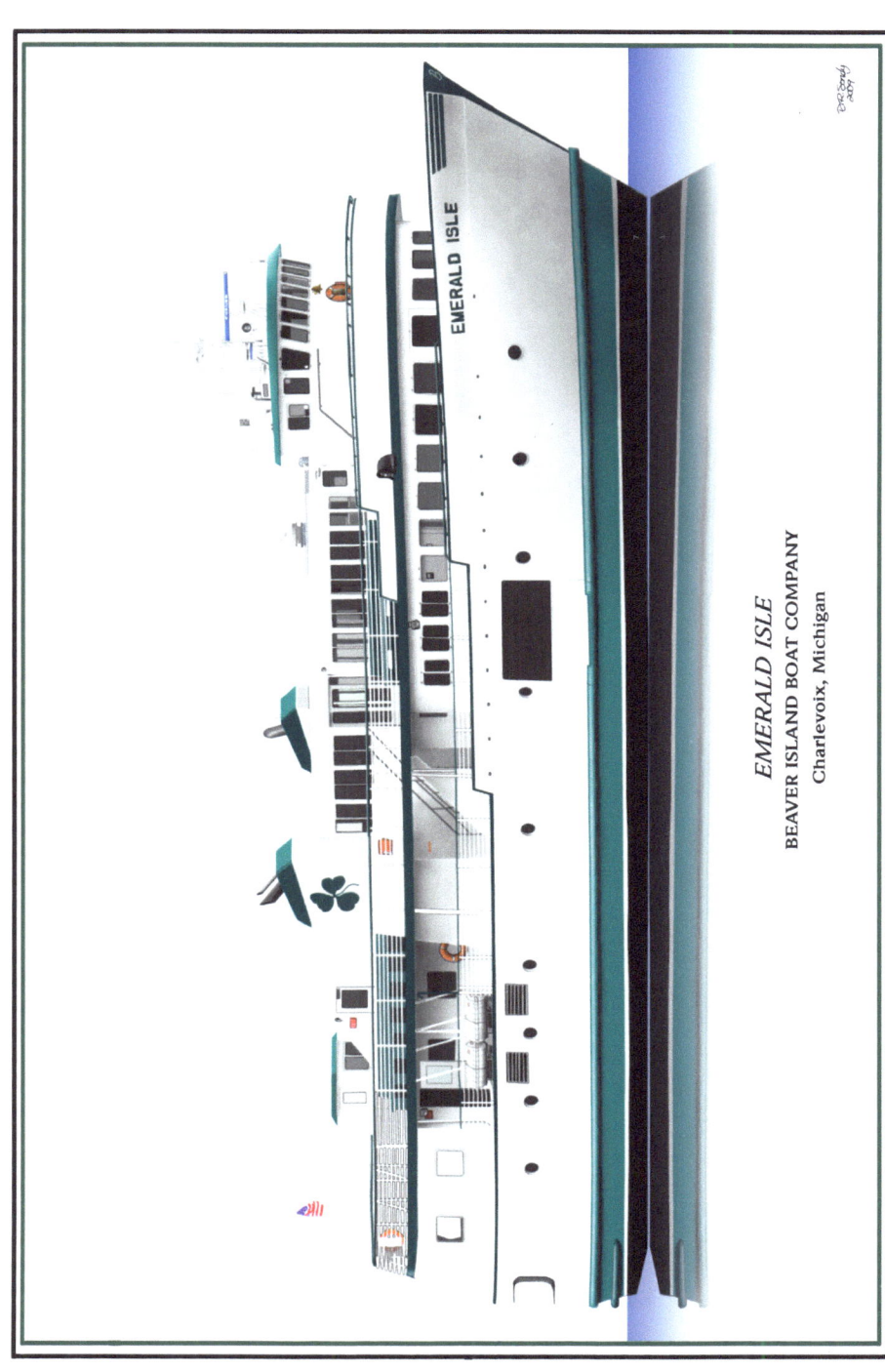

EMERALD ISLE
BEAVER ISLAND BOAT COMPANY
Charlevoix, Michigan

www.ingramcontent.com/pod-product-compliance
Lightning Source LLC
Chambersburg PA
CBHW041523090426
42737CB00037B/16